بِسْمِ اللَّهِ الرَّحْمٰنِ الرَّحِيمِ

Bismi Allahi Ar-Rahmani Ar-Rahimee

In the name of Allah, Most Gracious, Most Merciful

Good Manners in Islam

Contents:

Praise is to Allah the Creator of the world, the One Who exists without beginning, without end, without place, without how and does not depend on time, nothing is like Him and He is He Who hears and Who sees, whatever you can imagine Allah is different. And may the elevation in degree and the preservation of his community from what he fears for it be granted to our master Mouhammad Al-'Amîn, the Honest, the one who called for the religion of truth, Islam the religion of all the Prophets from the first 'Adam to the last Muḥammad.

Allāh tabāraka wa ta`ālā says in the honored Qur'ān:
"Qul hal yastawi alladhin yaelamun walladhin la yaelamun".

This means: «Say, Are those who know and those who do not know equal? » [Az-Zumar Ayah 9].

Saints, people of truth, faithfulness, purity, those who obey Allāh ta`ālā completely, scholars who work, who fear Allāh, who show piety, who prostrate and incline, who are embellished by good behavior, who have hastened to do good: they are embellished by good characters to lavish good. How much we ourselves, whether we are individuals or families, whether we are rulers or governed, how much it is fitting that we beautify ourselves by good behavior and that we run to do good.

It was reported in the ḥadīth of the Prophet that he replied to his companion Abu Dharr, may Allāh be pleased with him, by his honorable recommendations which elevate the degree of one who works with and attaches himself to it. Indeed, Ibnu Hibbân reported in his ṣaḥīḥ according to Abou Dharr, that Allāh is pleased with him, that he said: "My Beloved [Muḥammad] has recommended good behavior to me. He recommended me to look at the one who has less than me and not to look at the one who has more than me. He recommended me to love the poor, to get closer to them, and he recommended me to tell the truth even if it is bitter. He recommended that I maintain ties with people in my immediate family even if they have distanced themselves. He recommended that I say a lot: lâ Hawla wa lâ qouwwata 'il-lâ billâh (there is no strength to obey Allah except by His help and there is no protection against disobedience to Allah except by His protection)".

Good behavior, doing good, is part of the behavior of the Prophet `alayhi S-Salâtou wa s-salâm. `A'ishah, may Allah be pleased with him, said in the description of the Prophet: "He was not vulgar, he was not indecent, he was not one of those who raised his voice in the markets and he did not respond to the bad deed with a bad deed but he forgave".

- GIFT -

To thank you for your purchase, we would like to
offer you a free PDF copy that talks about fairness
and mercy in Islam.
You have just to send us a picture of that you have
purchased our book in this email:
aichasupa@gmail.com

The excesses of the tongue

"He who believes in Allah and the Day of Judgment, whether he speaks good or remains silent" (Bukhari)

Language, used in the context of speech, must be given special attention, as it is the main element of communication and relationship with the other. It is also a means of worshiping our Lord every day and in many ways, a tool that is both important and dangerous insofar as we must learn to take care of it, to control it and to make good use of it in order not to not become its victim. If in Islam the warnings against the excesses of the language are innumerable, it is clear that a large majority of Muslims still yield too easily to the temptation of this one.

This is how our master the Prophet warned the faithful against excesses of language. Talking can be very easy, and for many, words are less serious than actions. The error here consists in thinking that granting importance to what we say remains secondary and that the use of language, wrongly and through, is not in its sense very dramatic since "it does not remain just mere words".

However, we also know that words can be more hurtful than blows because words, unlike blows which only leave physical traces, directly affect the psychic and psychological state of the person. It is its interior and its stability that are thus affected. The Prophet describes the believer as "one who does not harm others either by his tongue or by his hand" (Bukhari). The Muslim can therefore in no way allow himself to neglect what comes out of his mouth. Allah has commanded us to be just and truthful even in our words when he says "How many generations have We destroyed after Noah? Your Lord is sufficient as Knower and Beholder of the sins of his servants" (surah 17; verset 53)

This is why you have to be vigilant, think before you speak and learn to measure the weight of each of your words. Very often silence is better. There is no doubt that underestimating the damage that our language can cause results in a fall into evil, the access to which is particularly easy in this era. This is why the Prophet said: "Whoever guarantees me what is between his jawbones and what is between his thighs, I guarantee him paradise" (Muslim). Holding your tongue and weighing your words can therefore seem quite difficult. Fortunately, no vice resists education. Lying, backbiting, slander.

These three words sum up the worst habits that occupy many discussions. Three things that can only lead away from the Lord. Indeed, regarding lies, Allah says: "Let us invoke Allah's curse on the liars" (s.3 v.61).

The Prophet adds: "Beware of lying, for indeed lying leads to perversion and perversion to hell. The man will begin to lie until he ends up being considered with Allah as a liar" (Bukhari). What could be more detestable indeed for those who claim to be Muslim not to take the side of the truth when the Quran tells us:

"O you who believe! Be conscious of Allah, and be with the sincere" (s.9 v.119).

As far as gossip is concerned, it presents a character that is both subtle and dangerous, which very often leads to confusion because the gossip is such that it pushes the people who practice it to believe that they are only stating a truth. , of course in evil, on a third party in his absence. Indeed, as the Prophet said, backbiting is: "To mention in the absence of a man what might displease him" (Muslim). For wickedness or levity in order to correctly assess the fact of slandering and thus understand how much the act is an abomination, it is enough to refer to the verse in which Allah tells us:

"O you who believe! Avoid most suspicion some suspicion is sinful. And do not spy on one another, nor backbite one another. Would any of you like to eat the flesh of his dead brother? You would detest it." (s.49 v.12).

Finally, slander consists in inventing things about a person and telling them to others at their expense. The finest proof of the vanity of slander remains the story of 'Aisha, when she was accused of having deceived the Prophet.

It was finally Allah himself who exonerated her and restored the truth:

"When you rumored it with your tongues, and spoke with your mouths what you had no knowledge of, and you considered it trivial; but according to Allah, it is serious" (s.24 v.15).

Wasting time causing harm to others remains above all unworthy of a person who says he wants to walk towards Allah. "Man can say a little word to which he gives no consideration while this one brings him closer to hell by seventy cubits" (Bukhari)

By adding, the small excesses that may seem insignificant on a daily basis but which are no less important, and cause harm to others, as well as to ourselves. We will cite, for example, insults and vulgarities of all kinds, which sometimes punctuate all the sentences of those who give them no consideration.

The exaggerations also, of those who transform the truth to attract attention, and the useless words, which contain no good and to which it would be wiser to privilege silence. Finally, the lack of discretion and modesty are particularly topical today. The Muslim must be discreet in his words, especially when they concern private life, or mistakes that are not to be boasted about. It is unfortunately nowadays quite common to go out and hear those who call themselves believers shamelessly display their misdeeds to get noticed.

They say that silence is golden and that you have to turn your tongue seven times in your mouth before expressing yourself, that's why preserving the language is certainly keeping one of man's worst enemies on a leash.

Education of the soul

"Successful is he who purifies it (the soul), Failing is he who corrupts it." (s.91 v.9-10).

This verse, among many others in the Holy Quran, brings man face to face with the primary goal, that of freeing himself from his ego and from any attitude contrary to the notion of servitude and devotion in which all aspiring to spirituality. The soul, therefore, needs an alchemy in order to preserve its first nature as Allah says: "So devote yourself to the religion of monotheism the natural instinct Allah has instilled in mankind. There is no altering Allah's creation. This is the true religion, but most people do not know." (s.30 v.30).

More than ever, the time has come for the reformation of souls, and the month of Ramadan, by the grace of Allah, is a unique occasion of its kind because, as our beloved the Prophet (saws) says: "If my community actually knew what the month of Ramadan entails, so no doubt they will wish that all the other days of the year were similar to Ramadan" (Al-Bayhaqi).

But before going further in the subject, it would be important for us to first know the soul and its realities as described in the Koran.

The Three Souls

By meditating on the verses of the Koran, we realize the existence of a certain form of classification of souls according to their ranks and their merits. Certainly, everyone is not at the same moral or spiritual level, there are some who are good and others who are less so, some who are very good and others even better as Allah says in a verse of the Koran: "They all have ranks according to what they did; and your Lord is not unaware of what they do" (s.6 v.132). Thus the Quran highlights three types of soul:

- **The soul called "Al Ammara" that is to say the ego.** It is the soul that advises only evil, passions and desires. Allah says: "Yet I do not claim to be innocent. The soul commands evil, except those on whom my Lord has mercy. Truly my Lord is Forgiving and Merciful." (s.12 v.53). This type of soul concerns those who are unfair to themselves because not only are they in the wrong but the darkening of their clairvoyance makes them hardly aware of the level of darkness of their station and therefore, they remain insensitive to any form of reminder "Those against whom your Lord's Word is justified will not believe, Even if every sign comes to them until they see the painful punishment." (s .10 v.96-97).

- **The soul called "Al Lawama" that is to say who regrets.** There are those who even, living in total darkness, still keep their consciousness which does not abandon them. They are often subject to self-criticism and questioning as Allah says: "And those who, when they commit an indecency or wrong themselves, remember Allah and ask forgiveness for their sins and who forgives sins except Allah? And they do not persist in their wrongdoing while they know" (s.3 v.135). In another verse Allah says: "Those who are righteous when an impulse from Satan strikes them, they remind themselves, and immediately see clearly." (s.7 v.201), that is what can be called "human consciousness". If there is a blame intended for this type of individual, it is the fact of reasoning after the act instead of doing it before.

- **The soul called "Al Motma'inna" that is to say serene.** The serenity of the soul is the desire of all spiritual. It is nothing other than the divinely granted faculty which has the effect of making the individual solid in his principles, flourishing in his actions and never allowing himself to be disturbed by any form of trial. These same individuals are therefore not inhabited by a deceptive conscience (Al Ammara) nor by a belated reason (Al Lawwama).

And it is with gratitude that their lord addresses them when he says: "But as for you, O tranquil soul, Return to your Lord, pleased and accepted, Enter among My servants, Enter My Paradise." (s.89 v.27-30)

Here, then, are the three different types of souls that can exist. Allah sums them up in another verse when he says: "Then We passed the Book to those of Our servants whom We chose. Some of them wrong their souls, and some follow a middle course, and some are in the foremost in good deeds by Allah's leave; that is the greatest blessing." (s.35 v.32)

Be yourself

The spiritual masters have made the search for the causes of sin one of their highest priorities because giving up sin through the body when the heart feels the desire and the taste is certainly a sign of a possible relapse. Hence the importance of attacking evil at its sources. Thus, some like Imam Abu Hamid Al Ghazali and many others, point to four characteristics which, because they are not compatible with the primary nature of man, are often the causes of his fall into the world of sins:

- The attitudes of the divine. That is to say that there are acts which are done only for the lord such as power, supremacy, eternity, pride, etc...

No need to learn the Koran to know that these remain the exclusivity of the divine, and when man wants to appropriate them, the result is unequivocal: "Pride is my coat and my pride is my pants, whoever tries to take it from me, I destroy it" (Muslim) and besides, what was the trick that brought Adam out of paradise? "Then the devil tempted him, saying, O Adam, shall I show you the Tree of Immortality, and a kingdom that never decays? (s.20 v.118).

- The characteristics of the devil. Man, when he wants to acquire certain characteristics which are totally divine, he goes astray just as when he imitates the devil in his vices, that is to say jealousy, tricks, hatred, racism, underestimating the other as when to justify his refusal to prostrate himself before Adam, Satan said: " He said, "I am better than he; You created me from fire, and You created him from mud" (S.7 v. 12) Here we have racism and discrimination in its most authentic form.

- Bestial characteristics That is to say, to have as concerns only the search for desire and the adoration of the passions like an animal in its quest for food and mating stripped of all reason. And when man lets himself be guided by his impulses instead of his reason, he then lowers himself to a level lower than the cattle as Allah says: "We have destined for Hell multitudes of jinn and humans. They have hearts with which they do not understand. They have eyes with which they do not see.

They have ears with which they do not hear. These are like cattle. In fact, they are further astray. These are the heedless." (s.7 v.179)

- The characteristics of predators. That is to say, everything that arises from anger, injustice or even the violation by force or constraint of the rights of others, hence the prophetic invitation made to men in order to make them masters. of themselves "The strong is not the one who defeats his enemy but he is the one who knows how to restrain his anger" (Bukhari).

Thus, man can only find his place and succeed in humanism.

There are very effective means in Islamic spirituality which, in a way, are the remedy for all these heart diseases. Hence the importance of referring to those experienced in esotericism, who knew how to put into practice the word of Allah "As for him who was defiant, And preferred the life of this world, Then Hell is the shelter, But as for him who feared the Standing of his Lord, and restrained the self from desires, Then Paradise is the shelter. (s.79 v.37-41)

Gold ring for men

Imam 'Ali, may Allah be pleased with him, reports that one day our master the Prophet, peace and salvation be upon him, put silk in his right hand and gold in his left hand then he said: "These are two things forbidden to men in my community. (Abu Daoud). Islamic law thus prohibits a man from having a ring, a watch or any other gold jewelry. It should be noted that this prohibition does not apply to women.

Eyebrow shaping

It is reported by Bukhari and Muslim that our master the Prophet, peace and salvation be upon him, formally forbade eyebrow waxing. This is unanimously recognized by the different schools. Exception made for any act of rectifying hair removal in the proper sense of the word, in other words when there is a manifest defect such as the two eyebrows which join or which grow abnormally. It must be understood by this that Islam is a follower of natural beauty and refuses the objectification of the human body.

Wearing the wig

Except for health reasons or related to constraints, wearing a wig is prohibited in Islam because according to Seyidna Ibn 'Omar, may Allah be pleased with him, as reported by Bukhari and Muslim, our master the prophet, peace and salvation be upon him , cursed those who wear a wig and those who wear hair extensions.

To dye one's hair

Imam Muslim reports according to Seyidna Jabir, may Allah be pleased with him, that during the capture of Mecca Seyidna Abu Qouhafa, the father of Seyidna Abu Bakr, may Allah be pleased with them. His hair and beard were white as snow. Our master the prophet, peace and salvation be upon him, then said: "Change this whiteness and avoid the color black". This hadith is the source that allows jurists to affirm three things concerning the fact of dyeing one's hair:

- It is recommended to dye your hair when it is all white.

- All colors can be used except black.L

- Older people are encouraged to accept who they are and not to cheat by pretending to be who they are not.

Tattoo

The tattoo in all its forms is banned by Islam for both men and women according to Seyidna Ibn Mas'ud, may Allah be pleased with him, our master the prophet, peace and salvation be upon him, said: " May Allah curse those who tattoo and those who get tattooed. (Bukhari)

Headscarf

The wearing of the veil is a divine prescription as it is clearly reported in verse 59 of sura 33: "O Prophet! Tell your wives, and your daughters, and the women of the believers, to lengthen their garments. That is more proper, so they will be recognized and not harassed. Allah is Forgiving and Merciful". As a result, sticking to this divine prescription does not depend directly or indirectly on her husband. Indeed, he has neither the right nor the power to impose on his wife not to wear or to wear the veil. Our Master the Prophet, peace and salvation be upon him, said: "No obedience to the creature to the point of disobeying the Creator" (Bukhari). And Allah The Exalted says: " There shall be no compulsion in religion " s.2 v256. But it may be that in situations, the woman is forced to choose between a divorce and keeping harmony within her family with her children, in this case, the union of families takes priority over wearing the sail.

Piercing on the nose and navel?

There is no clear source prohibiting piercing on the nose or the navel, so many scholars leave this practice to the taste of the culture and customs of each people even if personally, we do not lean towards this practice.

Women's perfume

Nothing prohibits women or men from wearing perfume and taking care of their body. The sources, which relate to certain restrictions, simply condemn the abuse which aims to draw attention or attention to oneself.

Modesty

"The sustainability of communities depends only on the safeguarding of morality".

These words of Imam Shafi'i give the key to community success, namely respect for morality. Good morals necessarily include basic rules of modesty and decency. Modesty is a characteristic trait that is first worked on individually. When a person has this character trait, it affects everything he does. Here, it is not only a question of clothing but also of the way of speaking, of holding oneself and of approaching others. Allah Most High declines modesty for each of our actions and each of our words. He details precisely how it should be translated: in the intonation of the voice: "And moderate your stride, and lower your voice. The most repulsive of voices is the donkey's voice." s.31 v.19; in our way of walking: "And do not treat people with arrogance, nor walk proudly on earth. Allah does not love the arrogant showoffs, And moderate your stride". (s.31 v.18-19)
In the way of looking: "Tell the believing men to restrain their looks, and to guard their privates. That is purer for them." s.24 v.30. Modesty is part of a lifestyle in its own right. Moreover, being modest means respecting one's being and only brings good, as the Prophet said: "Modesty, in all its aspects, is good" (Muslim).

On the other hand, it is important not to confuse modesty and false modesty. It is not about closing in on yourself, showing weakness or shyness. On the contrary, true modesty goes perfectly with asserting one's personality and taking responsibility for one's actions. In this regard, the mother of believers, Aicha, said: "What excellent women the women of the Ansars are, modesty did not prevent them from understanding their religion" (Muslim).

Unfortunately, today, modesty has become obsolete to the point of being listed as a fault. Yet more than ever, a return to values and spirituality is necessary at the risk of humanity. Each of us must begin this work of introspection and then extend it to our family, starting with our children, who are synonymous with the future.

Modesty and faith

Modesty is defined in Islam as anything that prevents us from indulging in reprehensible, blameworthy acts, turpitudes whose finality will only cause embarrassment and shame. Urging modesty therefore amounts to ruling out all forms of indecency. In order to better understand the importance of modesty within this religion and its place, we invite you to dwell for a few moments on the words of our noble Prophet Mohammed, peace and blessings of Allah be upon him: "Each religion has a ethics and the ethics of Islam is modesty".

You should know that modesty is innate in humans, over time either he will keep it and strengthen it or he will abandon it for lack of education. Our beloved the Prophet said: "Among the prophetic words that people have grasped are: If you have no shame then do what you want". No doubt he was trying to challenge Man to the fact that without shame, He would indulge in detestable and repugnant acts and gestures hated by Allah, His Messenger and men of good manners. Our beloved Master also said: "When Allah, Exalted be He, wants to annihilate a servant, he takes away his modesty. When he takes away modesty from him, he will only be detestable and odious, and loyalty will be taken away from him. When loyalty is taken from him, he will betray and be suspected of treason. When he betrays and is suspected of betrayal, mercy will be taken from him. When mercy is taken from him, he will be a stoned curse. When he is like this, Islam will be removed from him." On the other hand, He also says, thus emphasizing the inseparable nature between faith and modesty: "Modesty and faith go together, when one of the two disappears the other also disappears" (Bukhari) and: "The faith has seventy-something branches and modesty is a branch of faith" (Muslim). In other words, modesty is part of faith, so the more man strengthens his modesty, the more his faith increases. The converse also applies: the more his faith increases, the more He increases his modesty.

As a reward, Allah says: "And fear Allah, Allah teaches you" s.2 v.282. By acquiring modesty, the believer grants himself the noblest qualities of faith. This is not negligible because let us remember that faith is the essence of the life of the believer and especially that his life in the hereafter depends on it. Moreover, this prophetic word bears witness to this: "Modesty is a sign of faith. But faith leads to paradise. While obscenity is harm and harm to others leads to hell.

Modesty towards oneself

Although it is considered a humiliation or even an indignation for some, the dress of Muslim women remains in the realm of modesty. Islam applies the divine prescription: "They will be recognized more quickly and will avoid being offended". It should be noted in parenthesis that this practice is in no way an exception compared to other monotheistic religions, contrary to general opinion. But that is not the point, what matters to us here is to emphasize that the Muslim woman should not be limited to her headscarf! Especially since the current fashion-oriented trend betrays false intentions. The most convincing example is that of someone who wears a veil with extra-tight jeans and who, on top of that, absolutely does not respect her privacy, revealing her most obscene sins, when Allah had hidden them. Isn't that the height of the paradox?

According to Abu Horaira, the Messenger of Allah (blessings and peace of Allah be upon him) said: "All Muslims will obtain the remission of their sins except those who display their misdeeds. To exhibit one's misdeeds consists in exclaiming the next day, after having committed a fault during the night, when Allah has revealed nothing: "O so and so, I have done this and that...". While Allah had veiled his action all night, here he comes in the morning to exhibit the secret of Allah against him" (Bukhari).

What makes Man whether he is rich or poor, big or small, young or old, is: his morality. Thus was praised our Prophet by the Creator: "You are certainly endowed with noble qualities". Among these, the one that the Prophet considered to be the ethics of Islam: modesty.

The concept of happiness

Those of you who wake up in the morning in complete safety in your "sirb", in good health and having your daily subsistence, it is as if the happiness of this lower world has been served to you in its entirety. (Tirmidhi)

This wisdom is part of the prophetic treasures. Our beloved the Messenger of Allah, peace and blessings be upon him, has donated it to mankind in order to draw their attention to the essentials of Allah's blessings. Indeed, those who want to move forward must learn to observe those who preceded them among illustrious men in order to follow in their footsteps. However, in order not to fall into obscurantism which consists in ignoring the benefits of Allah to us, it is important to go back to the essentials. The believer must therefore look at the one who is above him to progress and the one who is below in order to thank his Lord and be grateful. It is in this sense that our beloved the Prophet said to our master Abu Dharr: "Look rather at the one who is below you! This is more likely to allow you to avoid minimizing the blessings of Allah upon you. (Al Hakim) Thus, this prophetic hadith comes to draw the attention of aspirants to the notion of earthly happiness. And like everything, it (the notion of happiness) can be increased or decreased.

As a result, our master Salama Ibn Oubeydillah Ibn Nihsan Al Khatmy, as Imam Bukhari tells us in Al Adab Al Mufrad and Tirmidhi, declares that he heard his father bring back from our beloved the Prophet this following word: "He among you who wake up in the morning in total safety in your "sirb", in good health and having your daily subsistence, it is as if the happiness of this lower world has been served to you in its entirety. Our beloved thus emphasizes three tenants of happiness which are peace and security, health and the minimum of subsistence.

Peace and security
The notion of peace, stability and security is a principle very dear to our religion. Thus, our Lord gave himself as attribute Peace, He says: "He is Allah; besides Whom there is no Allah; the Sovereign, the Holy, the Peace-Giver, the Faith-Giver, the Overseer, the Almighty, the Omnipotent, the Overwhelming. Glory be to Allah, beyond what they associate. (s59; v23). He made the believer's greeting an invocation wishing peace to his neighbour. Just as at the end of each prayer, peace is our ultimate invocation: "peace be with you". Facing the Lord, "Peace" will also be our first greeting on the Last Day. In this sense Allah says: "Their greeting on the Day they meet Him is, "Peace," and He has prepared for them a generous reward." (s33; v44)

On the other hand, our master the Messenger of Allah Yusuf found only peace and security to wish his family who came to live with him in Egypt. The Quran tells us: "Then, when they entered into the presence of Joseph, he embraced his parents, and said, "Enter Egypt, Allah willing, safe and secure! " (s12 v99)

All this to support the thesis that no success, no happiness, no project can see the light of day if there is no peace, security and social stability.And there is proof of the veracity of these say, the wars and the instability which reign in certain parts of the globe. Displaced populations, some entrenched in their homes, others killed, tortured or even terrorized, what place is there then for happiness? However, when the Prophet said: "Those among you who wake up in the morning in complete safety in their sirb", he used great wisdom. Moreover, the complexity of the word "sirb" and the immensity of the meanings that it encompasses pushed me not to translate it, so as not to restrict the hadith, because indeed, this word encompasses four different meanings in the Arabic language. It designates the person, the family, the path and the road as well as the house. As if our beloved the Prophet wanted to show us by the choice of this word, the moments when security is even more appreciated, namely to feel safe in oneself, in the midst of one's family, not to fear insecurity then that we are on the path and the road that leads to where we hope to gain something and finally to the heart of his home and his intimacy.

This hadith is then the proof of the veracity of the prophetic statement "my Lord has granted me bounty in speech" (Muslim), that is to say that in a few words it expresses innumerable meanings. When our beloved the Prophet emphasizes security, it is also a call to all believers to make peace and security their struggle. Besides external security, Allah promises us inner and spiritual peace. He says: "Those who believe, and do not obscure their faith with wrongdoing those will have security, and they are guided." (s6 v82)

Health

The second foundation of earthly happiness is none other than health in prophetic consideration. Health is an engine that allows Man to earn his living and to get closer to his Lord. No one can work to earn a living in complete serenity in the face of illness. Also, no one can easily discharge so-called "corporeal" religious obligations without health. Thus, health is a gift that must be preserved but it is also a goal that must be sought, and, in this sense, our beloved the Prophet puts us on this track on various occasions. He says: "Enjoy your health before illness" (Al Hakim). In another hadith he calls for food hygiene in order to preserve this health. He says in this sense: "The son of Adam cannot fill a vessel worse than his belly. If he is forced to do so, then he devotes one third to food, a second third to drink and the last third to his breathing. (Ahmad)

The daily subsistence

The last pillar of earthly happiness as described by our beloved the Prophet is none other than financial means. Indeed, living in dignity without reaching out to anyone must be accessible to all. The Koran is full of verses which repeatedly call for the restoration of social inequalities, human dignity, solidarity and sharing for all individuals. Moreover, for this fact, a pillar of Islam, namely the zakat, has been dedicated to this purpose. When we talk about living, we do not mean trivialities, waste, and everything that has the sole purpose of plunging societies into blind materialism. Didn't the Quran say: "Know that the worldly life is only play, and distraction, and glitter, and boasting among you, and rivalry in wealth and children. It is like a rainfall that produces plants, and delights the disbelievers. But then it withers, and you see it yellowing, and then it becomes debris. While in the Hereafter there is severe agony, and forgiveness from Allah, and acceptance. The life of this world is nothing but enjoyment of vanity." (s57 v20)

Our beloved used to say:

"O Lord, save me from hunger, for he is a bad fellow traveler and save me from betrayal, for he is a bad counselor" (Abu Dawood). This is how he views the danger to society; to let poverty prosper and gain ground as well as the degradation of values.

However, the true believer is not the one who, faced with a lack, despairs or seeks to satisfy it by any legal or illegal means. The true believer is the one who knows that in this lower world one cannot fulfill all his desires and the door of trial is always open and will not be closed for believers until after the return to their Lord. In this sense the Koran says: "Or do you expect to enter Paradise before the example of those who came before you had reached you? Adversity and hardship had afflicted them, and they were so shaken up, that the Messenger and those who believed with him said, "When is Allah's victory?" Indeed, Allah's victory is near."
(S2 V214)

He also says, "We will certainly test you with some fear and hunger, and some loss of possessions and lives and crops. But give good news to the steadfast, Those who, when a calamity afflicts them, say, "To Allah we belong, and to Him we will return", Upon these are blessings and mercy from their Lord. These are the guided ones."
(S2 V155-157)

And a thousand greetings to our master the Messenger of Allah who, in the face of trial, was the best example: "And mention Our servant Job, when he called out to his Lord, "Satan has afflicted me with hardship and pain.", "Stamp with your foot—here is cool water to wash with, and to drink.", And We restored his family for him, and their like with them; as a mercy from Us, and a lesson for those who possess insight, "Take with your hand a bundle, and strike with it, and do not break your oath." We found him patient. What an excellent servant! He was obedient." (S38 V41-44)

The Purity

Purification translates as **"tahara"** in Arabic and literally means: removing an impurity.

Islamic jurisprudence distinguishes two aspects: impurity and the state of impurity. Purification consists of getting rid of an impurity and changing a state called impurity in reference to bodily purity and spiritual purity. Note that the (material) impurity defiles only three elements: the body, the clothes and the place of worship. In Arabic, the word "wudu" literally means purity (or beauty). It is used to designate small ablutions (cf. §3.1 and §3.2). Legally, small ablutions consist of purifying well-defined limbs with water, some of which have been washed or over which one passes one's wet hands.

The merits

Concerning the merits of purification, we note the approval of Allah in the first place since He affirms in surah 2 in verse 222 to love those who repent and who purify themselves. Furthermore, our beloved master the Prophet said, "Whoever performs ablution and beautifies it, all his sins will leave his body even out of his fingernails." He also affirmed that Allah does not accept any prayer performed without ablution, hence the importance of purification.

The different ablutions: Wet ablutions
How to perform wet ablution?

Wet ablution (with water) consists of several steps, here they are in order:

- Brush your teeth if possible

- Mention the name of Allah: "Bismillahi rahmani rahim"

- Stand in the direction of Mecca if possible

- If an open container is used, stand to the right of the container

- Use only the bare minimum of water

- Wash your hands up to the wrists three times

- Wash your mouth using your index finger three times

- Wash the nostrils by inhaling and exhaling water three times

- wash your face three times

- Wash the forearms up to and including the elbows three times, starting with the right then the left.

- Run her wet hands through her hair

- Run your wet hands simultaneously over your ears

- Wash your feet up to your knees

- Pronounce the "shahada" to close the ablutions

It is tolerated to pass his wet hand on his shoes, during a next ablution, on the condition of having worn them immediately after his wet ablutions. This act can be repeated as many times as necessary for three days for the traveler and one day for the resident only if you have not taken your shoes off. In which case, it will be necessary before to redo its wet ablutions.

As for people who have bandages on one of the limbs concerned by the ablutions, they have three choices: either they perform their ablutions normally, excluding the limb covered with the bandage, or they pass their hand symbolically over it or finally they resort to dry ablutions.

Cancellation of ablution

It is important to know the elements that cancel ablution to avoid finding yourself in a state of impurity through ignorance.

The items that nullify ablution are as follows

- The vomit

- disbelief

- Loss of reason or epileptic seizure

- Fainting

- The exit of all substances or gases through the two orifices

- sexual pleasure

- heavy sleep

- Contact with a person of the opposite sex (at the Chafiite school)

- The doubt

- The blood

- The important gurgling of the belly

- The touching of one's sex (except in the Hanafi school)

- Everything that goes in and then comes out of the body

Dry ablutions

Called "tayamum", dry ablution consists of performing small or large ablutions without the use of water. They can be done only in case of lack of water or circumstances making it impossible or very difficult to use water.

How to perform dry ablution?

The process is simple, all you need to do is:

- Passing your hands over an earth element preserved in its natural form (sand, rock, etc.)

- Then pass his hands over his face and rub them each up to the wrists

There is another method practiced by Malikites and Hanbalites

- Run your hands over an earth element preserved in its natural form (sand, rock, etc.)

- Run your hands over your face

- Put your hands back on the item used previously

- Finally pass his hands over his forearms to the elbows

These two visions are valid since they are reported by the Prophet.

Note: In the event that one realizes that there is the possibility of performing ablution with water while one was performing the prayer with dry ablution, one must interrupt the prayer. then do it again after performing wet ablution.

The major ablutions

Allah says, "If you had intercourse, then purify yourselves" (S.5 v.6). Major ablution is performed as a result of one of the following causes:

Death, we then speak of mortuary washing.

After or before converting as desired.

After the total cessation of periods or lochia for women.

After ejaculation and whatever the circumstances.

After any penetration even if it is not followed by an ejaculation.

Apart from these cases, there are circumstances where it is desirable for the believer to perform great ablution such as:

- After performing a mortuary wash.

- Before the Friday prayer and that of the two major feasts.

- Before putting themselves in a state of sacralization for the pilgrimage.

Note: It is not necessary to redo the ablutions (wet or dry) after the great ablutions because they replace them. Certain rituals are prohibited when one is in a state of major impurity: prayer or tawaf around the Kaaba and reciting the Koran or touching it according to certain ulemas.

How to do great ablution?
There are two ways to do great ablution.
The first, the simplest, is to pass water all over your body, of course, with the intention of doing it for the major ablution ritual. The disadvantage of this method is the obligation to still make small ablutions before praying.

The second way is sort of a combination of showering and performing minor ablutions. In this way, one can perform the prayer without redoing one's minor ablutions. Here is how to do it:

- Wash your hands up to the wrists.

- Wash the part of his body between the navel and the knees at the front and at the back

- Wash your mouth, nose, face, hands to forearms once

- Wash your hair three times, making sure to wet it well, then your ears

- Wash your whole body starting with the right side then the left

- Wash his feet and between his toes

- Finally pronounce the "shahada"

The mortuary washing

The washing of the deceased is an obligation. It should be done as quickly as possible. It takes place exactly like the major ablutions. On the other hand, one must first close the eyes of the deceased, cut his nails, shave his pubic hair and those of the armpits, place him preferably on a raised surface, finally undress him, leaving his private parts covered. At the end of washing, we can braid the hair of the deceased if necessary.

Purification after his needs

It is mandatory to clean your private parts after defecating by any means, toilet paper for example, but it is preferable to use water for better hygiene (nothing prevents use both). Certain rules must be respected: take your time, start by washing the genitals before washing the anus in the case of stools, wash with the left hand. For the man do not touch his genitals with the right hand when he urinates.

Body cleanliness

Body cleanliness, in other words the maintenance of the growth of nails and hair, remains a prophetic recommendation. It consists of ensuring that you regularly wax your armpits and pubic hair, trim your mustache or beard, cut your nails and finally circumcise yourself.

Note: Eyebrow waxing is prohibited. On the other hand, waxing of the legs, back, chest, hands and feet is not prohibited for women. In men, it can represent a lack of virility.

Hair Removal Frequency: Anas says, "We have been given a 40-night frequency for mustache trimming, nail trimming, armpit hair removal and pubic hair shaving" (Reported by Muslim, Ibn Madja, Ahmad, Al-Tarmidhi, an-Nassai and Abu Dawood)

Veracity

Morality is unquestionably the essential foundation of the Muslim religion and the primary purpose for which the best of creatures were sent to us, peace and salvation upon him. The prophet says: "I was sent only to perfect the noble characters" Tabarani. Moreover, the value of a man, in Islam, is measured, not by his words and words, deeds and gestures, but by his morality.

In this sense, the prophet says: "Among the best among you, those who have the highest morality and the best character" Bukhari. Among these qualities making the nobility of man, determining the greatness of his convictions and the purity of his intentions vs with respect to his Lord, veracity. It is however necessary, in order to seize it in all its dimension, not to be mistaken as for the comprehension of the word veracity. Indeed, this virtue is not simply limited to saying a truthful word, but far beyond that, truthfulness is the act of aligning our apparent acts with those concealed. The exterior of man, what he reveals to other individuals, must not betray his most intimate convictions. Veracity is there, a state of total purity, a moral balance devoid of all forms of impurities in its intentions and of any behavior unworthy of what the faith claims.

By having understood this, we will be able to conceive the idea that will be and will remain a liar who affirms a truthful word without being convinced of what he says. Allah says in the Quran: "When the hypocrites come to you, they say, "We bear witness that you are Allah's Messenger." Allah knows that you are His Messenger, and Allah bears witness that the hypocrites are liars."
(s.63 v.1). Such is the judgment of Allah, the hypocrites do not lie on their attestation that our master Muhammad is the messenger of Allah, but their hearts do not share this reality affirmed by their language.

By meditating in the Qur'an, we can see that Allah has made this quality, truthfulness, one of his divine characteristics and attributes, He says: "And who speaks more truly than Allah? (s.4 v.87). In addition to being The Truth, Allah has assigned this indispensable quality to his prophets and messengers. Veracity is even one of their main qualities which Allah does not fail to recall several times in the Qur'an when quoting them: "And mention in the Scripture Abraham. He was a man of truth, a Prophet." (s. 19 v.41), or even "And mention in the Scripture Enoch. He was a man of truth, a Prophet."
(s.19 v.56). At the head of these noble messengers, there is the Prophet Muhammad, the one whose veracity was recognized long before his prophecy when the quraychis nicknamed him "The truthful and trustworthy" and reaffirmed during of the battle of the Combined when the believers, having seen the enemy coming in the same manner as the prophet had foretold them.

They said, "This is what Allah and His messenger have promised us; and Allah and His messenger have told the truth." (s.33 v.22)

Besides being a divine attribute, a characteristic of noble messengers, truthfulness is also an undeniable quality of true believers, Allah says about them: "Those who believe in Allah and His messengers these are the sincere".
(s.57 v.19)
Among these characters whose veracity was one of their distinctive signs, Seydatouna Mariam, this noble woman unique in her kind, who marked humanity and who is one of the four queens of paradise, Allah has summed up his behavior in a single qualifier: "The Messiah son of Mary was only a messenger, before whom other Messengers had passed away, and his mother was a woman of truth." (s.5 v.75). When we know that the prophet said: "Truthfulness certainly leads to piety and piety certainly leads to paradise. A man does not cease to be truthful until he is written as being a truthful " Bukhari, we can only act for the sole purpose of fighting the lie so that the truth will appear. Moreover, when we grant a little meditation to the divine word, we notice very quickly that the reward and the satisfaction of Allah will be granted only to the truthful, it is in this sense that Allah says: " Of the believers are men who are true to what they pledged to Allah. Some of them have fulfilled their vows; and some are still waiting, and never wavering, That Allah may reward the truthful for their truthfulness; and punish the hypocrites, if He wills, or pardon them. Allah is Forgiving and Merciful. (S.33 V.23/24)

As for the day of resurrection, Allah lets us know that protection against punishment will only be justified by this noble quality: " Allah will say, "This is a Day when the truthful will benefit from their truthfulness." "
(s. 5 v.119).
All these Quranic verses calling for good morality and more particularly veracity are supported by countless hadiths which all go in the same direction. Among these, the one in which the prophet says: "O Muadh know that no creature will testify that there is no other Allah but Allah and that Muhammad is His servant and His messenger, with a heart truthful, without it being preserved from the Fire". The Prophet says in another hadith narrated by Ubad: "Guarantee me six things from you and I will guarantee you paradise: Be truthful when you speak, do not break your promises when you promise, return what is entrusted to you, preserve your sex from any prohibited relationship, lower your gaze and do not cause harm to people". Ahmad

Among the many examples attesting to the great morality of our prophet, the testimony coming from his enemies. Abu Sofiane, a fervent companion who once fought the prophet, recounts: "when I was still in ignorance, at the time when I had the prophet as an enemy, I went to meet, at the request of Quraysh, the king of Byzantium seeking at home the uprising against the prophet. Hardly had I finished pronouncing my words, the Byzantine sovereign asked me the following question: "Was he known among you before this day as being a liar? answered him no, he was truthful and trustworthy until he said he had received the message of Allah. There the disbelieving ruler replied: "This man is right because it is impossible that a man who does not lie behind people's backs can utter lies about his Lord". This confirms the adage: "the truth sometimes comes from the mouths of its enemies".

Flirting

At present, some are wondering about the place of religion in this modern world. Is religion a brake or a motor? This question takes on its full importance when we approach sexuality or rather the relationship between man and woman in general. Between trying to get to know each other and remaining modest or even exchanging or fornicating the difference is sometimes very subtle for some.

It is about approaching flirting from an Islamic angle. Does Islam Ban Flirting or Regulate It? Is flirting necessary for the construction of a common project of complicity and love or is it simply a precocious enjoyment before its time? Before answering all these questions, it is necessary to recall here a basic rule to which Islam is particularly attached when it comes to love relationships, namely that the one and only regime that can govern the sentimental sharing of two sexes remains marriage. And the path that must lead to it must not strip it of all its meaning either.

Flirting: the key to temptation?

We meet, we like each other, we think that it is her or him the chosen one of our heart, so we do not hesitate to cross certain levels. From the tender and loving look through the gentle caress, we let ourselves slide towards kisses, which for the less daring will be the last step, but which, for the most determined, will open other doors more passionate than reasonable. And there, the wonderful idyll takes on another face, the rain replaces the good weather and we realize that we are too different or that we will never be able to get along. So we decide to end this story, which will give birth to a new story which will give birth to another until finally we resolve to ask ourselves if we do not pass for something much more than a being worthy of love and respect.

And it is precisely to combat the objectification of beings and submission to the passions that faith calls us to reason by these terms: "And do not come near adultery. It is immoral, and an evil way! ». (S17 V32)
Instead of "Do not fornicate", the formula "Do not approach fornication" or "do not come near" leaves something to think about. Failure to follow certain lifestyles can unfortunately become a bewitching spiral that will be difficult to get rid of. So, claiming that this way allows to know the person better and to guarantee a better durability of the future union is purely utopian.

Moreover, according to a study carried out by INED the divorce rate in France is constantly increasing, it reached an average of about 45% and amounted to 127,578 in 2009 against an average of 20,000 in 1914. This at a time when the present generations rejoice at the fall of the wall of modesty, but demonizing virtue will in no way lead to a moralization of vice: "Say: "The bad and the good are not equal, even though the abundance of the bad may impress you". (S.5 V.100)

Positive flirting?

That said, there is still a question that arises to know how to get to know the soul mate or are we condemned to marriage without loving each other? And if there must be sentimental love before marriage then how to build it? On this subject it is important to understand that for Islam, it is inconceivable that an enterprise of great importance such as marriage can be founded on the bases of doubt or ignorance. Otherwise what would be the scope of the divine word: "So that you know each other". Thus Islam, in its approach to moral sanitation, allows people of opposite sexes wishing to unite to first seek to know each other and learn to love each other. This, respecting the moral virtues that have been fixed on this subject. Imams Ahmad, Abu Daoud and Hakim report according to Jabir that our master the Prophet, peace and salvation be upon him, said: "If you want to marry a woman then, if you can, look in her for what could seduce you to the wedding ".

Then Jabir adds: "And when I wanted to marry a woman I hid to observe her until I saw in her what encouraged me to marry her and then I did". Imams Ahmad, Abu Daoud, Tirmidhi, Ibn Majah and Nasai report according to Moughira ibn Shou'bah that he wanted to marry a woman and that our master the Prophet, peace and salvation be upon him, said to him: "Seek at the see because it is what is more likely to put the agreement between you thereafter ".

All these sources demonstrate that there is nothing wrong with seeking to know your future soul mate while knowing that other sources determine the manner, the places and the limits of this process. On the other hand, the obligations of modesty and of our faith do not allow us to begin with the end.

The limits of flirting

Meeting, exchanging, working together, getting to know each other better or even showing one's attachment to the other in no way constitutes an offense to our faith. And the fact of advocating the strict separation between man and woman is on the one hand utopian and illusory, and on the other hand is nothing other than the fruit of an excess of zeal in the approach that you can have religion. Nevertheless, this relationship must be framed by the principles of morality, which are based on certain basic rules in order to guarantee purity and serenity, such as:

- **Modesty**: Whether in words or deeds, Allah Most High says in the Noble Qur'an: " If you observe piety. So do not speak too softly, lest the sick at heart lusts after you, but speak in an appropriate manner." S.33 V32. And our master the Prophet, peace and salvation be upon him, said: "If you are no longer modest then do what you want! (Bukhari)

- **Do not isolate yourself**: that is to say find yourself in three circumstances: Being alone, in a closed room, out of sight.

It is all the same important to remember that the believer must avoid all situations, even public ones, which could lead him to break the laws of morality and faith without, however, falling into a form of fanaticism or extremism which, in no cases, cannot lead to any success: "the practice of religion is easy and making it difficult leads to loss" (Bukhari).

Respect for human dignity and the sacredness of reason must be the best bulwark that prevents man from succumbing to temptation and becoming a slave to his impulses. And what a beautiful appeal to reason is the word of our Lord: "As for him who was defiant, And preferred the life of this world, Then Hell is the shelter, But as for him who feared the Standing of his Lord, and restrained the self from desires, Then Paradise is the shelter." (S.79 V.37 to 41)

The human

"We have honored the Children of Adam, and carried them on land and sea, and provided them with good things, and greatly favored them over many of those We created." (s.17 v.70)

It is by these words that the Koran defines, with precision, the position occupied by Man and the rank attributed to him among other creatures. As we meditate on this verse, we become aware of four divine gifts attributed to the children of Adam. The first favor concerns his dignity, his status: "We have honored the sons of Adam". The second is related to his freedom of movement, his living space: "We transported them on land and sea". The third relates to the power of detention: "We have given them good things". And finally, the fourth refers to his supremacy and his sacredness, which place him above all other creatures: "We have clearly preferred them to several of Our creations". This is the place of man. Long before voices were raised to defend the freedom, dignity, rights and sacredness of human beings, the Koran by the voice of His Lord and the demonstration of the Messenger had illustrated what the fight of the men for men.

We honored the sons of Adam

Reading this verse, one may be led to wonder about the way in which Allah has honored Man. The answer can be summed up in three points: The Lord honored him by giving him life. Indeed, the just fact of having allowed man to exist proves an inalienable right to life and to respect for his choices. Our Prophet, peace and salvation be upon him, used to say man is the work of Allah and woe to him who undermines the work of the latter. The Koran goes even further by decreeing that whoever kills a soul or sows terror on earth, it is as if he had killed all of humanity and whoever allows a soul to live in dignity, c It is as if he had given life to all of humanity.

The gift of reason

To return to the divine honor given to Man, we can cite the reason for which he gave him. Which of course differentiates him from animals, as they say: "Man is a thoughtful animal! ". On the other hand, Allah in the Qur'an has blamed so much those who do not work their intelligence, He says: " We have destined for Hell multitudes of jinn and humans. They have hearts with which they do not understand. They have eyes with which they do not see. They have ears with which they do not hear. These are like cattle. In fact, they are further astray. These are the heedless.» (s.7 v.179)

Precisely we will answer those who support the theory according to which: it is necessary to believe without asking questions, that the Koran has considered reason as proof of faith and this in more than a hundred verses. Moreover, the expression "Do not reason" has been repeated twelve times in the Koran and seven times with the formula "So that you can reason". And is there a better answer than the Prophet, who affirms that: "faith is exempt for all people who no longer have reason" (Muslim). On the other hand, as the spiritual masters recommend, it is important to remain vigilant so that passions do not take over reason.

Free will

The third honor is none other than free will. Human choices must be respected as long as they do not harm the general interest and do not encroach on the freedom of others. Nobody can therefore force someone to do anything, and especially not to believe or not to believe. Unlike the angels, whom Allah designed to submit to His will (innately and automatically), He left the choice to man. Allah says in the Quran: "Whoever wills let him believe. And whoever wills let him disbelieve". (s.18 v.29) He also says "We guided him to the way, be he appreciative or unappreciative." (s.76 v.3)
Undoubtedly, it is preferable to blind faith, a desired and chosen belief. Allow me to add that Islam is far too dignified to impose itself on men. It only comes through in the lives of the faithful to the extent of their involvement.

Remember it is men who need a Lord and not the other way around! And to all those who take themselves for the ministers of the Divine and who seek to impose their doctrine on others, we let the Koran answer them with these verses: "Do they not see how We deal with the earth, diminishing it at its edges? Allah judges; and nothing can hold back His judgment. And He is quick to settle accounts." s.13 v. 41, "Will you compel people to become believers?". (s.10 v.99)

This constraint should not even be moral and the refusal of a man to faith does not justify the refusal to assist him: "And if anyone of the polytheists asks you for protection, give him protection so that he may hear the Word of Allah". (s.9 v. 6)

There is no good in a doctrine, even a religious one, if it does not allow man to awaken the humanity that lies dormant in him. He does not belong to the faith who does not give esteem to the work of Allah. We certainly have the best example in our Messenger Muhammad, peace and salvation be upon him, when seeing a funeral procession pass in front of him, he stood up with dignity as a mark of respect and compassion for the pain of the one to whom we takes a loved one. And when his companions pointed out to him that this deceased was not a Muslim, he answered them insistently: "Isn't that a soul? ". And during the victory of Mecca, he only said to his enemies of yesterday: "Go, you are free".

Humanism is also morality!

In conclusion, I would like to share with you a hadith of our beloved, the Prophet, peace and salvation upon him, in which addressing his disciples, those who have embraced the faith, he explains to them the moral identity that every believer must build in him: "My Lord has ordained me nine great qualities: sincerity in public and in private, truthfulness in joy and anger, modesty in wealth and poverty, to forgive those who wronged, to go to him who refuses to come to me, and to give to him who once refused me his support, to make my words an act of adoration, my silence a meditation and my gaze a observation ".

(At Tabarani)

Servants of the All-Merciful

It is with pleasure that we meet today in this Friday reminder to see together the identity of the believer as defined by the Quran. The character of those whose deeds our Lord has called honorable and their testimony of faith true.

This theme is important insofar as it tends to shed light on the definition of the Muslim's commitment to religion at a time when, unfortunately, humanity is undoubtedly living through a dark hour in its history. We certainly live in an era marked by the collapse of human values and the loss of orientation. Evil has become honorable and good subject to accusation. However, as our Lord said so well: "Say: The bad and the good are not equal, even though the abundance of the bad may impress you".
(s.5, v.100)

Thus, by meditating on the verses of the Koran, and more particularly on the sura "Discernment", we see that it is closed by about fifteen verses which only have for but to bring clarifications and discernment between the servants of the All-Merciful and the servants of the passion. For it is time to recognize that claiming to have faith does not mean having faith. By meditating on the last verses of the sura "Discernment" we see the Lord attribute to true believers in their commitment fifteen qualifiers, none of which can escape the globality.

Before going into the analysis of these moral attributes, let's first look together at the beauty of this text.

"The servants of the All-Merciful are those who tread the earth with humility and when the ignorant turn to them, they say peace. Those who pass the nights prostrate and standing before their Lord; those who say: O Lord, remove from us the punishment of Gehenna, its punishment is indeed lasting, and what a bad place to dwell! Those who when they spend neither waste nor are stingy but stand in the middle ground. Those who do not invoke any other deity with Allah and who do not kill the soul which Allah has made sacred except with good reason, and who do not fornicate - whoever indulges in this will incur punishment.

The torment will be doubled for him on the day of Resurrection and he will remain there eternally covered with ignominy. Apart from those who have repented and done good deeds, these are those whose bad deeds Allah will change into good ones, Allah is indeed Forgiving and Most Merciful. He who repents and does good, it is to Allah that his return will end. Those who do not give false witness and who, when passing trifles, pass with dignity; those who when reminded of the signs of their Lord do not become deaf or blind. Those who say, "And those who say, "Our Lord, grant us delight in our spouses and our children, and make us a good example for the righteous", Those will be awarded the Chamber for their patience, and will be greeted therein with greetings and peace, Abiding therein forever—it is an excellent residence and destination. (s.25, v.74-76)

These are the verses that highlight the fifteen attributes that make up the identity of the believer.

1. Humility

"The servants of the All-Merciful are those who tread the earth with humility." Treading the earth with humility, as it is quoted in this verse, in no way means simply paying attention to your step, it goes far beyond that, it is a way of saying that true believers are those who do not allow themselves to be corrupted or tempted by the cult of the ego, they are humble in their encounters, humble at work, humble in the reasons for their travels and the means of these, humble because the greatness of the earth constantly reminds us of the smallness of their being. In this sense, Allah says in another verse: "And do not walk proudly on earth. You can neither pierce the earth, nor can you match the mountains in height."
(s.17, V.37), and nothing can invite more humility than to know that earth we were created, in the earth we will return and from it we will come out.

2. The believer does not waste his time

"And when the ignorant speak to them, they say peace." It is an invitation made to believers to reason with them on the misdeeds of sterile polemics, especially when it turns into a dialogue of the deaf whose interlocutor is nothing but an ignoramus. This is not a call to despise the ignorant, but an invitation to guard against the risks that this can cause.

And the best way to guard against the ignorance of others is to embody a single word: peace. A way of saying: leave it up to the ignorant to call for hatred, and combat his hatred by advocating peace; leave him his pleasure in polemics, and jealously preserve your happiness in keeping peace.

3. Asceticism

"Those who pass the nights prostrate and standing before their Lord. " Is this not an invitation to the Islam of the contemplation of the hearts, the Islam of enjoyment of the soul, the Islam of spiritual happiness, as our beloved the Prophet said so well: " my own happiness is found in prayer". It is very surprising to see that in today's world, the practice of Islam simply stops indexing the other and comparing oneself to the most morally deprived, thus forgetting the great part of the communion between the human and divine for which religions have been enacted.

4. No to future humiliation

"Those who say: O Lord, remove from us the punishment of Gehenna, indeed its punishment is lasting, and what a bad place to dwell!" They seek protection from hell and fear it only because it is a reflection of divine dissatisfaction and the wrath of the Lord. Likewise, they desire paradise only because it reflects the satisfaction and love of their Lord.

Seen from this angle, we can then understand that the believer can experience hell or paradise on earth, depending on his ties with his Lord.

5. No to excess

"Those who when they spend do not waste nor are stingy but stand in the middle". There are not only two ways between lust and avarice, there is the measure, this measure which is nothing other than the balance which allows the believer to discern the weight of each thing and the part which must be assigned.

6. Pure worship

"Those who do not invoke any other deity with Allah". The error into which the majority of Muslims fall today is to think that associationism boils down to prostrating oneself for a statuette, forgetting that our beloved the Prophet warns us against what he likes to call subtle associationism. He also said in this sense: "the smallest portion of ostentation is associationism because whoever does this has placed humans in the rank of a divine who deserves that we dedicate our actions to Him. »

7.   Stop the blood

"And which do not kill the soul which Allah has made sacred except with good reason". Because they understood that Man is sacred because being the work of Allah, and cursed be he who attacks the work of Allah. In another verse of the Quran, Allah lets us know that killing a soul is equivalent to erasing all mankind from existence.

8.   Chastity

"And who do not fornicate". If Allah forbids this act, it is to give moral hygiene to humanity, to guarantee filiation and the stability of a life based on fidelity and mutual love.

9.   Veracity

"Those who do not give false witness".
This verse raises a doctrinal question, namely: how to judge the admissibility of the one who attests to the uniqueness of Allah, if the lightness with which he approaches the meaning of testimony in his everyday life is proven?

10. No futility

"and when they pass trivialities, pass with dignity". The ulama approach this verse by giving it as an explanation all that can be considered damage to the tongue, such as backbiting and slander, but this verse also shows the loftiness and excess with which the believer must respond to the blameworthy.

11. The sensibility

"those who, when reminded of the signs of their Lord, become neither deaf nor blind. Many people claim faith, but when it meets their passions and desires, they behave like the deaf who have not heard the word, or a blind man who has never seen the signs. Such is not the believer.

12. Start with your family

"Those who say: 'O Lord give us joy in our wives and descendants. To achieve this joy for the eyes, it is important to have recourse to two things: the right choice of soul mate and the good transmission of values to our children.

13. Exemplary

"And make us guides for the pious". The believer must always be the best example, wherever he is, in his morality, his servitude before his Lord, when he acts and when he abstains, he must always be a source of inspiration for the souls in search of discernment.

Sura "Discernment" is the scale that allows you to measure the degree of your Islam, imploring the Lord to grant us the strength to stick to righteousness every day.

The heirs of the book

By having given guidance to men, our Lord has once again shown the need for everyone to have a divine light to give meaning to the inner light that is in us, that is to say the faith. Thus, faith alone is not enough if it is not given a framework in which it can evolve and flourish. This framework is nothing but the Islamic message represented by the Quran and the Sunnah.

Each believer must, for this purpose, rejoice at having been chosen to be one of the beneficiaries of this extraordinary message. Indeed, it is the choice of Allah that is in question. In this sense, Allah says: "Then We passed the Book to those of Our servants whom We chose." (35:32).

As this verse states, men do not react in the same way to receiving this divine message. Some were more receptive and therefore experienced bliss.

Some others welcomed him with less enthusiasm while others, by the weakness of their commitment found themselves facing themselves and therefore facing a certain loss, if not the grace of their lord. who catches them. Thus Allah clearly states: "Then We passed the Book to those of Our servants whom We chose. Some of them wrong their souls, and some follow a middle course, and some are in the foremost in good deeds by Allah's leave; that is the greatest blessing." (S35 V32) It is with clarity and in everything explained that Allah, through this verse, puts his finger on a fundamental element, namely the diversity of reactions of everyone in the face of guidance. Thus, the Lord shows us the three different paths that have been taken by his creatures. The first reaction expressed in this verse is that of an individual who harms himself "There are some among them who harm themselves". The second "who stand on a middle way", are they qualified as being middle. As for the third category, it is that of the elite.

The unfair to himself

Going back to the first category, "There are some among them who wrong themselves", first referred to in this verse is the one who is unjust to himself. The latter is the holder of the so-called "Ammara" soul, that is to say that his misfortune lies in his conscience which never questions and, rather than questioning it, he pushes it in its error as it is said in the Koran: "The soul commands evil".
(12: 53).

In reality, someone who finds himself in this situation finds himself without spiritual or moral reference, even if all day long he does not stop claiming to belong to the community of faith. How many are those who, through their actions, have never ceased to demonstrate the flagrant paradox between what they are and what they claim to be. However, the Lord did not quote them to condemn them but, on the contrary, the All-Merciful quoted them in order to help them see better what they are and what they should be. There is therefore no room for fatalism or despair and as Muhammad Al Boussiri said: "O soul, do not despair because of the greatness of your faults because the sins faced with the extent of the forgiveness of the Lord lose their weight". Better still, he also says: "rather than despair, be convinced that the shares of mercy distributed will be according to the need of each one. »

The way

As for the second category, after the unjust towards themselves, the Koran qualifies them as being average people. More clearly, they are in the happy medium between the elite and their opposite. If the unjust to themselves abstain from the appeal of practice, the "means" fulfills all its obligations concerning its religion. He makes sure to behave in the most exemplary way, but his main characteristic that earns him the "passable" rating is that from time to time he weakens, he bends and lets himself be influenced by temptation.

But that does not immediately prevent him from pulling himself together and showing his regret before getting back on the right track. On this subject, Allah says: "Those who are righteous when an impulse from Satan strikes them, they remind themselves, and immediately see clearly." (7:201).

Unlike the unjust who sees his conscience playing tricks on him, the "average" only sees weaknesses in his actions; deep down, he is always called to adoration by his conscience. Besides, this is why Allah in the Qur'an calls it "the self-blaming soul" (75:2).

The proof of his belonging to this category has been clearly expressed in the quoted verse of surah Imran and which groups together three conditions: repentance after the act, remembering Allah after the moments of carelessness and finally, once the reason returned, never to start the sin again. Allah says: "And those who, when they commit an indecency or wrong themselves, remember Allah and ask forgiveness for their sins—and who forgives sins except Allah? And they do not persist in their wrongdoing while they know, Those—their reward is forgiveness from their Lord, and gardens beneath which rivers flow, abiding therein forever. How excellent is the reward of the workers." (S3: V135/136)

One who works for good

The verse of Sura Fatir, as we have seen, has shown everyone's position in the face of righteousness. He called some unjust to themselves, others 'means', and then comes the third category of people: 'and others with Allah's leave precede [all others] by good deeds ", and "he who works together in good" is nothing other than he who has no concern or aspiration but to merit the approval of his Lord. The path taken by the latter is the path of excellence. Where some no longer know where they are and others maintain themselves in constancy, men of excellence flourish in the happiness of an unfailing and unconditional devotion to their lord. And what better example to illustrate these people than Abu Bakr, the one who in the midst of the companions, the prophet asked: "Who among you is fasting today? No one answered in the affirmative except Abu Bakr. The Prophet asked, "Who among you visited a sick brother today?" Umar replied, "O Messenger of Allah, we have just finished the dawn prayer. How could we have done it? Abu Bakr humbly replied, "I, O Messenger of Allah. I learned that `Abd Ar-Rahmân Ibn `Awf was sick and I went to his house before coming to the mosque. The Prophet asked, "Who among you gave alms today?" 'Umar replied, "O Messenger of Allah, we have just performed the prayer and have not yet left our places.

Where could we have come across a poor man to help him? Abu Bakr replied: "On my way to the mosque, I met a needy man. Finding a piece of bread in my grandson's hands, I gave it to him. The Prophet said: "O Abu Bakr, you are the man who surpasses everyone by competing in good, Paradise is announced to you as good news.

(Ibn Kathir)

Prophetic advice

We meet around a hadith of our beloved prophet, peace and salvation be upon him. This hadith, reported by Imam Tirmidhi, may Allah have mercy on him, in his collection of Sahih, relates that one day, the companion Abu Dhar Al Ghafari came to see the Prophet, peace and salvation be upon him, to ask him for a advice. Abu Dhar then said: "Oh Messenger of Allah, advise me", the Prophet, peace and salvation be upon him, replied: "Fear Allah wherever you find, follow your bad deeds with good ones in order to erase the bad ones. , and behave with people in the best way".

This hadith is part of the so-called "jawami'il kalim" hadiths; this means that the Prophet, peace and salvation be upon him, addresses people with very wise phrases and using few words. This ability is one of the unique characteristics of the prophet. Thus he says in a hadith:
"I received six merits compared to other prophets: I was given concise words with a lot of meaning, I was rescued by fear, the booty was allowed to me , the earth was given to me as a purification and a place of prayer, I was sent to all creation and it is through me that the number of prophets ended" (Muslim).

"Fear Allah wherever you find, follow up bad deeds with good ones, so you will erase the bad ones, and behave with people in the best way". In this hadith, the Prophet teaches Abu Dhar the behavior that the Muslim must have sometimes with his lord, sometimes with himself and sometimes with his fellow men.

Fear Allah wherever you are

The prophet begins with the relationship that must exist between man and his lord, he says: "Fear Allah wherever you find". The fear of Allah is manifested in the believer by the force enabling him to put a barrier between him and the disobedience of Allah. If he is tempted to lie, he remembers that Allah says: "Woe to you on that day, to the liars". If a woman passes in front of him, he remembers the word of Allah: "Tell the believing men to restrain their looks, and to guard their privates. That is purer for them. (S24 V30).

When his parents make a remark or a reproach to him, he will act in accordance with the verse: "do not say to them a word of disrespect, nor scold them, but say to them kind words, And lower to them the wing of humility, out of mercy, and say, 'My Lord, have mercy on them, as they raised me when I was a child'.'"
(S17 V23-24).

Thus the fear of Allah rhymes with the feeling of the divine presence at all times.

The fear of Allah is not a word that claims only; but it is the art of putting a barrier between you and anything that can lead to the wrath of Allah. In other words, we can say that the fear of Allah is a companion or a friend that always guides you towards the best behavior to have in any situation. Therefore, if this feeling is rooted deep within man, all doors of divine mercy, sustenance, knowledge, blessing will be wide open to him.

Follow bad deeds with good ones

In the second part of the hadith, the Prophet highlights the habit that every holder of faith must have, when the bad sides of his soul take over reason, or when he has committed excesses vis-à-vis of himself. This habit consists of not letting despair get the better of you and that the disappointment of having made mistakes does not prevent you from rectifying them. Allah says in this sense: "and do not despair of Allah's comfort. None despairs of Allah's comfort except the disbelieving people." (12:87). Indeed, the attitude to have after committing a sin is not to feel sorry for oneself. There is also no question of not regretting the harm that has been done. But instead of living in despair, man must rather rectify his error by increasing acts of good. Thus the Prophet said: "Fear Allah, wherever you are", and when you do evil, follow it up with good deeds, so you will erase the bad ones.

Thus a man at the time of the Prophet, peace and salvation on him, had actions unworthy of a Muslim vis-à-vis a woman. Then, after coming to his senses and realizing the gravity of the act, he came to the Prophet in tears and full of fear, complaining about his situation, not knowing how to react. Allah then sent down a verse from the Surah Houd intended for anyone seeking to redeem themselves from their sins, Allah said: "Perform the prayer at the borders of the day, and during the approaches of the night. The good deeds take away the bad deeds. This is a reminder for those who remember." (11:114)

Deal with people in the best way

As for the third and last part of the prophetic advice, it concerns the relationship which must exist between man and his fellows; the Prophet said: "Behave with people in the best way". Such are the teachings of our religion, because the Muslim is he whose neighbor is harmed neither by his tongue nor by his hand. Thus the Prophet said: "The one I love most among you and those who will be closest to me on the day of resurrection are those who will have the best morals" (Ahmad). He says in another Hadith: "The Muslim can achieve the greatest degree of worship among those who fast and those who watch at night, simply by good morality. (Abu Daoud). This reminds us of the words of the emir of poets, Ahmed Chawky when he said: "Communities exist only through good morality, and when this disappears from them, they disappear with it. »

The spiritual journey

During Ramadan, the simple fact of seeing the number of Muslims increase in the mosques is proof of the authenticity of the divine word which says, speaking of the month of Ramadan and its characteristics: "the month of Ramadan during which the Koran was sent down as a guide for the people, and clear proofs of the right direction". And the attachment or the consideration of Men for their religion is part of these clear proofs of the guidance which comfort us to always affirm that all the good lies in the reconciliation of Man with his conscience.

Despite all this, this does not prevent us from asking ourselves some questions about this enthusiasm and this fervor that revolve around the coming of the month of Ramadan. Is it really a starting point that coincides with a real desire to walk towards Allah? Or is it a deception of the soul, insofar as you devote much more importance to secondary elements at the expense of essential things, you lean more towards the branches than towards the root? This question is very relevant as we are in a time when people are rushing more to do the tarawih prayer together at the mosque, than they would for the obligatory prayers of maghreb, isha, dhohr, asr, let alone of the fajr prayer.

All this shows one thing; the misunderstanding of people as to why the month of Ramadan has come, the spiritual significance of the month of Ramadan. It is a month of abstinence, both from food and moral baseness. It is a month of rapprochement with Allah and moral education in order to purify our souls so that they are better than before the coming of Ramadan and continue to improve after the end of Ramadan. But this cannot happen if we do not review the basics of the path to Allah, or how to best apply the verse that says "flee to Allah".

The first step is to repent sincerely towards Allah, to express the sincere will never to fall back into past faults. So that you can only conceive of happiness or success after having repented as Allah says: "And repent, all of you, O believers, in order to know success".

If you make this commitment, the second step is to respect the obligatory things, not only to respect but also to beautify. Step by step. Once you make your prayers on time, put before you the prophetic word "man will not be rewarded for his prayer except in the times in which he was concentrated". Nothing can be built or fortified unless the foundations have been consolidated as they should be.

You will then understand that to attach more importance to supererogatory acts than to obligatory acts is nothing but a deception of the soul, and to neglect obligatory acts in order to respond to the satisfaction of such or such is a total lack of discernment. This is why it is said in a hadith qudsi: "My servant has not approached Me by a better act than those which I have made obligatory on him".

The third step is to choose additional or supererogatory acts that you will not only respect, but which in addition will be up to your faults because the purpose of these forms of worship is to educate your soul and to fight your faults. . Each act is a drug that must be chosen according to the illness of each and every one. Thus, the Companions frequently posed the question to the Prophet: "Which is the best worship?" or "what is the deed most loved with Allah?". What is interesting to note is the fact that the Prophet, peace and blessings be upon him, gave as many different answers as he was asked questions. He says to a companion: "it is the fact of being regular in your actions", to another he says: "the fact of bringing joy into the heart of the Muslim", to another he answers: "don't don't get upset". To another he says: "Perform the prayer at its time", to another he replies: "Pilgrimage accepted". All these answers for a single question: "what is the best action?" Hence the need to choose the drug according to the one who asks for it.

Finally, after complying with the divine will, there is one last thing: to last over time. Worship is not restricted to the month of Ramadan; on the contrary, if we want to know if the month of Ramadan has been beneficial to us, we must see if today we continue to observe the adorations that we did a month before. The month of Ramadan was intended to accustom our bodies to fasting, praying, invoking, giving...

In order to make it a habit all year round. Regularity in worship is the main characteristic of al istiqama. It determines the sincere will of the believer; it is certainly easy to wake up once in the middle of the night and invoke Allah. Doing it regularly... that is al istiqama. The quantity does not matter, what matters is the regularity. To sum up the way the Prophet worshiped Allah, Seydatuna Aisha said: "His deeds were regular and constant". The Prophet, peace and salvation be upon him, said himself: "The best work with Allah is that which lasts even if it is small in quantity".

Prophetic recommendations

In a previous section, we had seen together the beginnings of the farewell sermon delivered by the prophet, peace and salvation be upon him, during his last pilgrimage. After having evoked the importance of his last recommendation, we continue in the dissection of this final message, constituting probably the testament of the messenger of Allah for his community.

Accounts to be rendered

"Remember that in truth you will meet your Lord and that indeed He will call you to account for your deeds. »

Through this message, our master the prophet, peace and salvation be upon him, reminds people of the inevitable encounter with their Creator. This meeting marks the balance sheet of each individual in life here below, which will be drawn up on the Great Day. Whatever the status of Man in this life, divine equity will be the balance of his acts leaning either for a life of eternal enjoyment if good animated him, or for the punishment symbolized by divine wrath if evil prevailed over his work. In this low world, it happens that Man can escape justice, because it is carried out by Men themselves. Families who are victims of atrocities committed by criminals can therefore be harmed by the sanction taken by the courts. Sometimes, the perpetrator of crimes can even escape sentence due to a lack of required evidence or the absence of witnesses. It is a fact, man is not perfect. But this will not be the case on the day of accounts. The witnesses, this day, will not be missing. Allah had indeed assigned to each person two angels responsible for registering and testifying to his actions. "As the two receivers receive, seated to the right and to the left, Not a word does he utter, but there is a watcher by him, ready. (S50 V17/18).

Each of the facts and gestures will be subject to the Judgment. Allah says in this sense: "On that Day, the people will emerge in droves, to be shown their works, On that Day, the people will emerge in droves, to be shown their works, And whoever has done an atom's weight of evil will see it." (S99 V6-8)

All these Quranic and prophetic warnings aim to push the human being to have a view of self-control. The prophet, peace and salvation on him, announces this message at a time when everything is clear in matters of religion; the good and the bad are illuminated and detailed in such a way that Allah will reveal at the end of this farewell sermon: "Today I have perfected your religion for you, and have completed My favor upon you, and have approved Islam as a religion for you. ". (S5 V3)
So there are no more excuses. Everyone is now responsible for their actions and liable to be judged.

The economic system
"Allah has forbidden you to practice usury, so any unpaid interest will now be waived. Your capital, however, is yours. You will neither inflict nor endure any injustice. Allah has decided to make the interest unlawful, and any interest that was due to Abbas ibn Abd'al Muttalib will now be cancelled. »

After having thus evoked the sacredness of Man and his goods, the prophet, peace and salvation upon him, continues in the moral and human continuity of his speech by prohibiting usury. Little by little, this practice became definitively banned. Islam has always condemned usury but has gradually banned it.

In the Quran, several verses refer to usury. Indeed, the first verse to be revealed on this subject is the following: "The usury you practice, seeking thereby to multiply people's wealth, will not multiply with Allah. But what you give in charity, desiring Allah's approval—these are the multipliers." (S30 V39)

This verse, revealed in Mecca, explains, by way of introduction to the judgment which will be given on the interest, the immoral side of it. Immoral because it aims to enrich oneself at the expense of others. Although this verse did not clearly prohibit usury, it nevertheless showed that this practice is not acceptable with Allah. As for the three other verses revealed on this subject, they were revealed in Medina, after the Hegira, each verse more explicit and condemnatory than the previous one. The following two appear in Sura The Women: "Due to wrongdoing on the part of the Jews, We forbade them good things that used to be lawful for them; and for deterring many from Allah's path, And for their taking usury, although they were forbidden it; and for their consuming people's wealth dishonestly. We have prepared for the faithless among them a painful torment."
(S4 V160/161).

These two verses come to approve the first by denouncing this practice of usury authorized by the previous peoples in this case the Jewish people.

...ectly to believers by categorically ... using interest: "O you who believe! ... on usury, compounded over and over, and ... so that you may prosper." (S3 V130).

... this verse, all ambiguity disappears. Moreover, Islam calls us to always consider forbidden what is immoral. Usury is cynical because it is contrary to mutual aid, solidarity and constitutes a brake on social stability. Unfortunately, the whole world, including Muslims, uses the interest rate banking system. Worse, Muslim states are among the most corrupt in terms of economy.

Today, everyone denounces this economic system, involving usury, which is at the root of the crisis we are experiencing, but no one offers an alternative. Each Muslim therefore tries individually to get rid of it in their expenses while waiting for the financial model adapted to Islamic teachings. The seriousness of usury is such that this sin is mentioned among the last verses revealed to the Prophet, peace and salvation be upon him: "Those who swallow usury will not rise, except as someone driven mad by Satan's touch. That is because they say, "Commerce is like usury." But Allah has permitted commerce, and has forbidden usury. Whoever, on receiving advice from his Lord, refrains, may keep his past earnings, and his case rests with Allah. But whoever resumes—these are the dwellers of the Fire, wherein they will abide forever, Allah condemns usury, and He blesses charities. Allah does not love any sinful ingrate.
(S2 V275-276)

And Allah say: Those who believe, and do good, and pray regularly, and give charity—they will have their reward with their Lord; they will have no fear, nor shall they grieve, O you who believe! Fear Allah, and forgo what remains of usury, if you are believers, If you do not, then take notice of a war by Allah and His Messenger. But if you repent, you may keep your capital, neither wronging, nor being wronged, But if he is in hardship, then deferment until a time of ease. But to remit it as charity is better for you, if you only knew, And guard yourselves against a Day when you will be returned to Allah; then each soul will be rewarded fully for what it has earned, and they will not be wronged."
(S2 V277-281)

For more books and exercise books, activities or coloring books in Arabic or Islamic, please visit our author page: **"Aicha Mhamed"** You have also found a book that talks about the history of Islam, Ramadan and others.